Defining MOMENTS
OVERCOMING CHALLENGES

Ray CHARLES

Find Another Way!

by Susan Sloate

CONSULTANT
Thomas Leitch
University of Delaware

BEARPORT
PUBLISHING

New York, New York

Credits
Cover and title page, © AP Photo/KEYSTONE, Franco Greco; 4, Ed Jackson;
5, © Eudora Welty/Corbis; 6, © Michael Ochs Archives.com; 7, © National Archives;
8, © Brown Brothers; 9, © Universal/Photofest; 10, © Brown Brothers; 11, © Universal/
Photofest; 12–13 (both), © Courtesy of the Florida School for the Deaf and Blind;
14, © Michael Ochs Archives.com; 15, © Lloyd Sandgren/Silver Image; 16, © Gossie
McKee; 17, © Michael Ochs Archives.com; 18, Photo: Ed Jackson; 19, © MPI/Getty
Images; 20L–20R (both), © Schomburg Center for Research in Black Culture, The New
York Public Library, Astor, Lenox and Tilden Foundations; 21, © Keystone Features/
Getty Images; 22, © Robert W. Kelley/Time Life Pictures/Getty Images; 23, © Flip
Schulke/CORBIS; 24, © Bill Ray/Time Life Pictures/Getty Images; 25, Photo: Ed
Jackson; 26, © Bureau L.A. Collection/CORBIS; 27, © AP Photo/John Hayes.

Publisher: Kenn Goin
Project Editor: Lisa Wiseman
Creative Director: Spencer Brinker
Original Design: Fabia Wargin

Library of Congress Cataloging-in-Publication Data

Sloate, Susan.
  Ray Charles : find another way! / by Susan Sloate ; consultant, Thomas Leitch.
    p. cm. — (Defining moments/Overcoming challenges)
  Includes bibliographical references and index.
  ISBN-13: 978-1-59716-267-8 (library binding)
  ISBN-10: 1-59716-267-1 (library binding)
  ISBN-13: 978-1-59716-295-1 (pbk.)
  ISBN-10: 1-59716-295-7 (pbk.)
  1. Charles, Ray, 1930–2004—Juvenile literature. 2. Singers—United States—
Biography—Juvenile literature. 3. Blind musicians—United States—Biography—
Juvenile literature. I. Leitch, Thomas M. II. Title. III. Series: Defining moments (New
York, N.Y.)

  ML3930.C443S56 2007
  782.42164'092—dc22

                                          2006005221

For more information, write to Bearport Publishing Company, Inc., 101 Fifth Avenue,
Suite 6R, New York, New York 10003. Printed in the United States of America.

10 9 8 7 6 5 4 3 2

Table of Contents

The Worst Seats

Blind musician Ray Charles and his band got off their big touring bus. They had just reached the concert hall in Augusta, Georgia. That night, Ray expected to play for his fans, who loved his swinging **rhythm and blues** music.

The Bell Municipal Auditorium in Augusta, Georgia, where Ray was scheduled to play

However, the **promoter** told Ray that the audience had to be **segregated**. In the 1950s and 1960s, black and white people weren't allowed to sit together in the concert hall. Black audiences, Ray's most faithful listeners, had to sit high up in the balcony. These were the worst seats. Ray didn't think it was fair.

Until the mid-1960s, many places in the United States kept black and white people separate in schools, public bathrooms, and restaurants.

In the South, and in some other states, black people had to buy theater tickets at segregated ticket counters.

Ray Fights Back

Black people came to Ray's concerts, bought his records, and loved his music. He thought they deserved better seats. He suggested that they sit closest to him and the white people sit in the balcony. The promoter said no. In the South, white people always had the finest seats.

Ray Charles and his band

Ray always wore dark glasses to protect his eyes from dust and pollen.

Ray decided that he and his band wouldn't play in Augusta. It was wrong to force his best fans to take the worst seats.

The promoter reminded Ray that he had signed a **contract**. "If you don't play," the promoter said angrily, "I'll **sue** you!"

"Go ahead," Ray said calmly.

Growing Up Poor

Ray knew he would find a way to fight the promoter. As a child, Ray had learned not to give up when times were tough.

Ray was born on September 23, 1930, in Albany, Georgia. Soon after, he and his mother, Retha, moved to Greenville, Florida. His brother, George, was born in this poor country town.

Albany, Georgia, where Ray was born

Ray's interest in music began when he was about three years old. Mr. Pit, who owned a local restaurant, taught him how to play the piano. Ray spent hours practicing. He loved making his own sounds.

Ray liked to listen to **jazz**, **swing**, and country-western music on Mr. Pit's **jukebox**.

Mr. Pit teaching Ray to play the piano in the movie Ray (2004).

Troubles

Ray and George played together while Mama did other people's wash to earn money. One day, George fell into Mama's big washtub and couldn't get out. At first, Ray thought that George was fooling around, but he wasn't. Before Ray could get help, George drowned. He was only four years old.

When Ray was a child, many women, like his mother, did other people's laundry in order to earn a living.

Unfortunately, there was more sadness to come. A few months later, Ray noticed a cloudy liquid in his eyes. He had to wash it out every morning. In a few months, Ray could hardly see. The doctor gave him some medicine, but it didn't help. Ray began to go blind.

Ray's blindness may have been caused by an eye disease that strikes mostly children.

In this scene from the movie Ray (2004), Ray's mother talks to her son about losing his eyesight.

Darkness

By the age of seven, Ray could see only shadows. Yet Mama would not let him feel sorry for himself. She wouldn't let other people help him, either. She told him, "There's always another way to do something if you look for it. Find another way!"

Children arriving at the school Ray attended for deaf and blind students.

Using a guide dog or a cane can help blind people get around. Ray never used either. He just depended on his great memory.

Mama made Ray do chores at home so he could learn to be **independent**. She taught him to use his memory instead of his eyes to guide his hands as he worked. Soon, however, Ray couldn't see at all. Mama decided to send him to a school for the deaf and blind in St. Augustine, Florida. Alone, Ray traveled hundreds of miles (km) by train to get there.

Though the students worked hard, there was also time for some fun at Ray's new school.

Learning to Cope

At school, Ray missed his mother, but he got used to being away from home. He learned to read **Braille**. He was taught to make mops and chair bottoms so he could earn a living. Most important, Ray studied music.

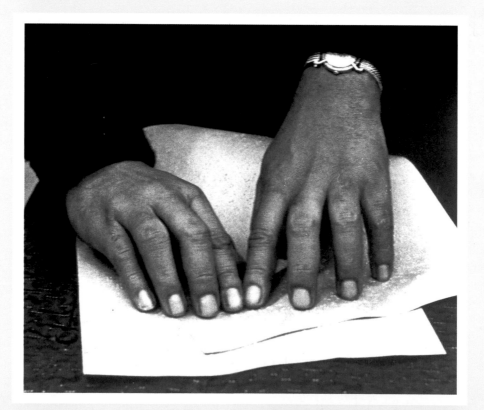

Ray reading Braille as an adult

In school, at about age ten, Ray learned to write and **arrange** music in Braille.

Ray spent summers at home with Mama. During his vacations, he played piano and sang with local bands to make money. In 1945, when Ray was about 15 years old, Mama died suddenly. Now Ray was alone. He decided to quit school and move to Jacksonville, Florida, to work as a musician.

Ray playing the saxophone during a performance in Jacksonville, Florida

Starting Over

About a year later, Ray moved to Seattle, Washington. He started a band and began to record his own music. He also had a local television show. Everyone loved his rhythm and blues music. They packed clubs to hear him. Ray became a well-known musician in Seattle.

Ray's first band, the McSon Trio

Ray recording an album for Atlantic Records in about 1951

Ray changed his name from Ray Robinson to Ray Charles. He didn't want people to confuse him with the boxer Sugar Ray Robinson.

Ray's records began to sell well. He started to travel with his band. However, because he was black, he was often not allowed to stay in some hotels or eat in certain restaurants. Still, he kept working, writing more songs and testing out new sounds. Soon, he became famous around the country.

Facing the Music

At the time Ray refused to play in Augusta, millions of people were fighting to end segregation. They were working hard so that black people could get the same rights as white people. Ray hadn't joined the fight yet. He was spending his time writing songs and touring the country.

Augusta, Georgia, in the 1960s

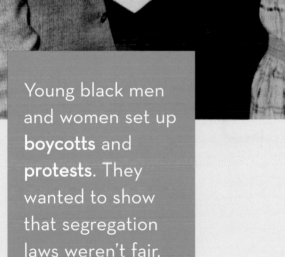

Young black men and women set up **boycotts** and **protests**. They wanted to show that segregation laws weren't fair.

This group of people staged a "sit-in" in Nashville, Tennessee, to protest segregated lunch counters. At the sit-in, black protestors sat down and refused to move.

As he had promised, the promoter sued Ray. Ray decided that he would fight back. He knew his case would be tough to win. Though separating black and white people was wrong, it was still legal in Georgia and other states. A judge might decide that Ray had broken the law.

The Verdict

When they went to court, the promoter said Ray had broken their contract. He wanted to be repaid the money he lost when Ray refused to play. Ray said he was protecting his black fans. He felt laws separating black and white people were wrong.

At Request Of Students

Blind Troubador Cancels Segregated Georgia Date

AUGUSTA, Ga. — Singer - bandleader Ray Charles canceled an appearance here at Bell auditorium Wednesday night after learning that he was to appear under segregated conditions.

Students at Paine college had earlier sent a telegram informing him of the situation. However, as it was not sent to the correct hotel in Atlanta on Sunday, Mr. Charles, "The Blind Troubador" did not receive the message until Wednesday afternoon after he had arrived in Augusta.

The telegram said, "The students at Paine college have some reservations as to your knowledge of the conditions under which you will perform here Wednesday night at Bell auditorium. We are presently urging Negroes not to support segregated affairs. The dance floor is open only to whites and Negroes are allowed only as spectators in an opposite auditorium." The wire was signed: Student Body, Paine college.

ON WEDNESDAY afternoon, a representative of the student body contacted Tom McGarrity, pilot of Mr. Charles' private plane, to confirm a report that the performance had been canceled. He informed the representative that Mr. Charles had checked with the promoter and found that the segregated conditions were true. They immediately [...] Augusta.

"I feel that it is the [...] that I can do to stand [...] my principles and h[...] students in their fight [...] principles."

Wife Of Col[...]

RAY CHARLES Says 'No' To Bias

He'd Rather Pay Than Play

RAY CHARLES Won't Eat "Crow"

Ray Charles Fined; Would Not Bow To Georgia Jim Crow

Special Correspondence
AUGUSTA, Ga.—Early this week, volunteer signature-gatherers had collected some 8,500 names on petitions saying "We Can't Stop Loving You" which will be sent to singer-bandleader Ray Charles.

The cause for "love" of the singer locally is the manner in which he had his lawyers to handle a judgment brought against him by a dance promoter.

(Another Story On Entertainment Page)

[...]moter. The singer hurriedly and happily told his lawyers to pay it off.

IN FULTON Civil Court at (See RAY, Page 2)

Ray's battle with the promoter made newspaper headlines.

While he was fighting his court case, Ray also formed his first big band. The Ray Charles Band had about 20 players, with many brass instruments.

The judge ignored Ray's protest about segregation. He saw only that Ray had not honored his contract. So the judge ordered Ray to pay more than $2,000 to the promoter.

Ray was one of the first performers to challenge the unfair laws. Though he lost the case, his actions encouraged other famous people to join the fight.

Joining the Fight

The court battle made Ray think more about the **civil rights** movement. He saw that people like Dr. Martin Luther King, Jr., were trying to change the unfair laws. Ray admired Dr. King and his peaceful marches and protests.

Dr. Martin Luther King, Jr., (middle) along with fellow protestors during the March on Washington

On August 28, 1963, almost 250,000 people, both black and white, joined Dr. King's March on Washington.

During the March on Washington, Dr. Martin Luther King, Jr., gave his famous "I have a dream!" speech.

Ray decided to get involved. However, he couldn't join the marches. There were some people who didn't like Dr. King or his ideas. They might throw glass bottles and other dangerous things at the marchers. Since Ray was blind, it wasn't safe for him to walk with the others. Instead, he helped raise money for Dr. King. He also refused to play any concerts that were segregated.

Back to Georgia

Ray never let his **disability** get in the way. In the 1960s, he built his own recording studio in Los Angeles. He recorded more than 300 songs there. Sometimes Ray even drove a car. A friend who could see sat beside him and told him what was on the road ahead.

Ray was able to play chess on a board that was specially made for blind people.

In 1979, Ray was finally welcomed back to Georgia. At a statehouse ceremony, he got a **standing ovation**. The governor apologized for the state's segregation laws. Then Ray sang his **signature** song, "Georgia on My Mind."

In 1979, "Georgia on My Mind" became the state song of Georgia.

Ray plays "Georgia on My Mind" for the Georgia House of Representatives.

Brother Ray

Ray stayed busy to the end of his life. He played his music all over the world. He was loved everywhere he went. Ray appeared in many movies and commercials that introduced him to new, younger fans. He also recorded songs with many famous singers and musicians.

Musical legend Frank Sinatra called Ray "the only genius in the business."

In the early 1990s, Ray performed in a series of popular commercials for Diet Pepsi.

On June 10, 2004, at the age of 73, Ray Charles died. He left behind hundreds of songs and millions of fans who called him Brother Ray. His music moved people of all ages. Though Ray's life hadn't always been easy, Ray never gave up. He always found a way to make things better.

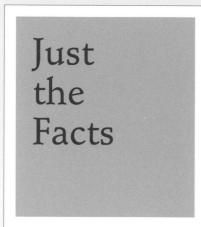

Just the Facts

■ The school Ray went to as a child taught both deaf and blind children. Yet the students were separated by race, not by disability.

■ For years, Ray had a group of female singers in his bands. He called them the Raelettes.

Timeline

Here are some important events in Ray Charles's life.

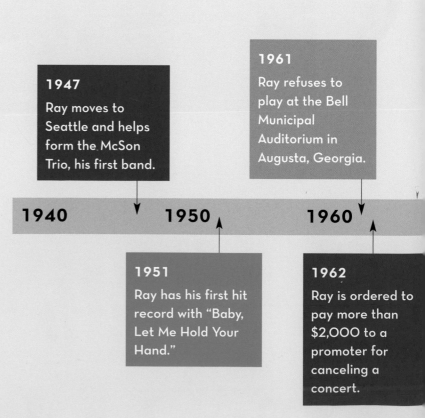

1947
Ray moves to Seattle and helps form the McSon Trio, his first band.

1961
Ray refuses to play at the Bell Municipal Auditorium in Augusta, Georgia.

1940   **1950**   **1960**

1951
Ray has his first hit record with "Baby, Let Me Hold Your Hand."

1962
Ray is ordered to pay more than $2,000 to a promoter for canceling a concert.

■ Ray's songs were a mix of jazz, rock, pop, blues, and country-western music.

■ Ray was married twice. He had 12 children and 20 grandchildren.

■ Ray played chess against people who could see. He won by remembering the setup of the chessboard and every move that he and the other player made.

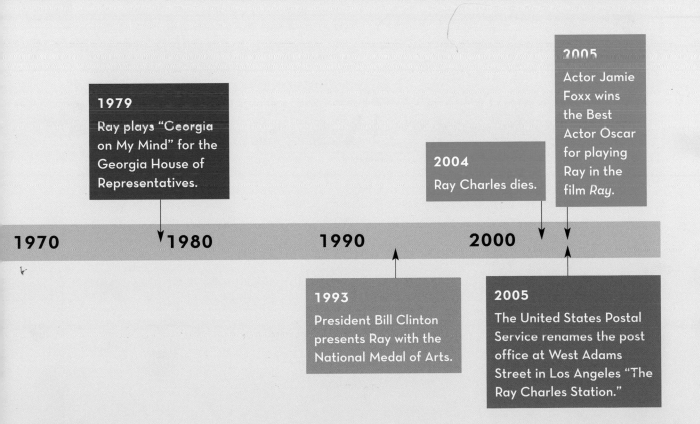

1979
Ray plays "Georgia on My Mind" for the Georgia House of Representatives.

2004
Ray Charles dies.

2005
Actor Jamie Foxx wins the Best Actor Oscar for playing Ray in the film *Ray*.

1970   1980   1990   2000

1993
President Bill Clinton presents Ray with the National Medal of Arts.

2005
The United States Postal Service renames the post office at West Adams Street in Los Angeles "The Ray Charles Station."

Glossary

arrange (uh-RAYNJ) adapt musical notes for different instruments

boycotts (BOI-kots) acts of refusing to buy or use something to make a protest

Braille (BRAYL) a system of raised dots on a page that are arranged in certain ways to spell out words for blind people to read using their fingertips instead of their eyes

civil rights (SIV-il RITES) in the United States, the rights people have under the law, such as the right to vote and the right to equal, fair treatment

contract (KON-trakt) a written agreement between two people that tells them how much one of them will be paid to perform a certain job

disability (*diss*-uh-BILL-uh-tee) a condition that makes it hard for a person to do everyday things

independent (in-di-PEN-duhnt) free of control from others

jazz (JAZ) a type of music that has interesting rhythms and is often played by groups of four to six musicians

jukebox (JOOK-boks) a machine that plays music after you put money into it

promoter (pruh-MOH-tur) a person who sets up the details of a music or artistic performance

protests (PROH-tests) demonstrations against something

rhythm and blues (RITH-uhm AND BLOOZ) a type of music especially well known in the South, often played on the guitar or the piano

segregated (SEG-ruh-*gay*-tid) set apart or separated from others

signature (SIG-nuh-chur) something an artist is best known for

standing ovation (STAN-ding oh-VAY-shuhn) people standing up to applaud

sue (SOO) to take someone to court to solve a problem

swing (SWING) a type of lively music played in the 1930s and 1940s, usually by a big band

Bibliography

Charles, Ray, and David Ritz. *Brother Ray: Ray Charles' Own Story.* Cambridge, MA: Da Capo Press (2004).

Lydon, Michael. *Ray Charles: A Man and His Music.* New York: Taylor & Francis (2004).

Read More

Beyer, Mark. *Ray Charles (Rock & Roll Hall of Famers).* New York: The Rosen Publishing Group (2002).

Ritz, David. *Ray Charles: Voice of Soul.* New York: Chelsea House (1994).

Turk, Ruth. *Ray Charles: Soul Man.* Minneapolis, MN: Lerner Publications (1996).

Learn More Online

Visit these Web sites to learn more about Ray Charles and his music:

www.pbs.org/wnet/americanmasters/database/charles_r.html
www.raycharles.com
www.swingmusic.net/Ray_Charles_Biography.html

Index

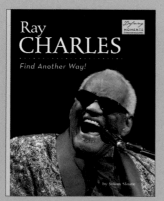

About the Author

SUSAN SLOATE is the author of many young-adult books and an adult novel, *Forward to Camelot*. She lives outside Charleston, South Carolina.